Don't Forget to Claim Your

FREE Training

Taught Personally by Adam Gower Ph.D.

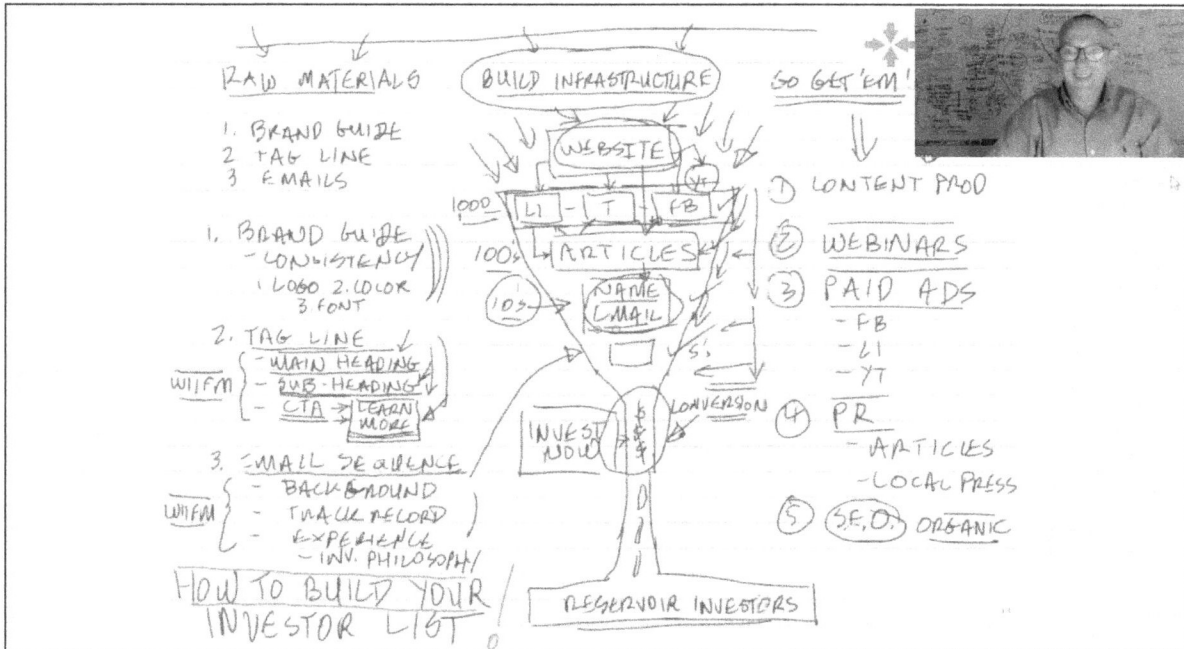

<< Click to Register Here for Immediate Access >>

Or go here:

hub.gowercrowd.com/syndicate-webinar

Table of Contents

A Personal Note From Adam Gower

The Real Estate World Has Changed

The man who has a thing to sell,
And goes and whispers it down a well,
Is not so likely to collar the dollars,
As he who climbs a tree and hollers!

Henry Taunt, 1902

The world has changed.

Real estate finance is being transformed, as so many industries before it, by a transition to the online world and I wrote this book to help you benefit and thrive from these changes.

It is written to give you the tools you need to build your reputation, to be seen, to be heard, to be trusted by more investors, to be recognized as an industry leader and to raise as much money for your projects as you could possibly ever need.

And the biggest discovery you will make when you implement what you learn in this book, is that raising capital has never been easier.

Investors will be attracted to you as a center of gravity for their investment dollars… they will see you as an authority and will be presold on your deals before you even pitch them.

Follow the tactics, techniques, and systems in this book and your entire money raising effort will be made easier, faster, and more effective.

You'll spend less time *financing* your deals and more time *finding* them.

The Era of In-Person Networking is OVER.

No more tedious networking at the country club, foundation, or association in the random hope that you might just bump into an investor.

Never wine and dine prospects again.

No more two-hour pitch meetings to raise equity for your deals.

When you follow the blueprint laid out for you in this book, you won't have to go out searching for investors: *They will come to you.*

You will convert prospects into active investors, active investors into repeat investors, and repeat investors into advocates for you, recommending your deals to their friends, relatives and colleagues.

AN EXTRAORDINARY OPPORTUNITY

Until recently the only way you could raise money for real estate was in-person from people you already knew.

But now you can reach out to every investor ONLINE.

Think about the sheer power of that for a moment.

Before you would have to make one phone call to one person one at a time. Now you can post one message on LinkedIn, Facebook, Twitter or any number of other social media platforms, and the whole world can see it.

And that's totally free.

You can send emails to thousands of people at once, you can advertise to hyper-targeted groups of your ideal investors, you can hold webinars in front of hundreds of investors, or go on podcasts to pitch to thousands of prospects, **all who have *asked* to listen to you and who are glued to your every word.**

And guess what…

Investors WANT to invest in real estate online

Not only do they *not* want to sit with you for hours while you pitch them on your background, track record and upcoming deals, but even if they did, they simply cannot due to Covid.

Even when the pandemic is in the rear-view mirror, investors will have become **accustomed to finding deals online** and making their decisions remotely.

> You have a tremendous advantage because your competitors haven't figured this out yet.

They have always wanted to know how to invest in real estate and now they want that delivered to them at their convenience, when they want it, without a pushy developer trying to coax them into investing.

And this gives you a tremendous advantage because your competitors haven't figured it out yet. They still think all they need is a website that acts like a fancy business card and that capital raising is still done in in-person meetings.

Once you've set up the MACHINE you're going to learn how to build in this book, you'll not only be making life easier for yourself, but *you'll be making it easier for your investors too because…*

Investors also want you to tell them *HOW* to invest

Remember the last time you bought something online for a few hundred dollars? What was the first thing you did?

Research.

You researched the product to educate yourself. You read reviews, and spent time making sure you were making the right decision before hitting the **BUY NOW** button.

And it is extremely unlikely that you actually talked or met with someone at the company selling you the product.

We have all become used to buying stuff this way and real estate investors are no different; they also do research before investing - *especially as their checks are in the tens of thousands of dollars or more.*

They *want* to go online, read everything, learn everything, get to know about you and your deals and to be taught how to understand the finer points. In short, they want EDUCATING on the process and the more they can get educated, the more comfortable they feel making the decision to invest.

It is exactly the same as before – only now, instead of being educated in person by the sponsor raising the money, they want it all delivered to them ONLINE.

Make it easier for your prospects to invest by simply giving them what they want!

It just doesn't take that much to make life easier for your prospects and to jump ahead of everyone else out there trying to catch the eye of these same investors.

What you're getting in this book is a ***blueprint*** for creating a powerful, investor attracting, lead generating, educational online presence with automated emails built into it that will make raising money easier for you, and investing easier for your prospects.

You're getting an *Investor Acquisition System* that will enhance your visibility, build your reputation as an industry leader, and will draw investors to you magnetically, pointing them to YOUR investments and predisposing them to invest with you.

So, let's get on with it.

Adam

Part I: The Way Forward

What you're going to be learning are three of the core pillars to raising more money online for your projects by **automating the process** so you can get on with finding more deals while investors gravitate to you without you having to go out to find them.

This is a detailed, actionable book that is going to leave you with some brand-new skills that you can *immediately put into action.*

So be ready to get started implementing what you're going to learn today as soon as you're done reading – it's going to change everything you do for the better.

The more things change, the more they stay the same

Check this out.

What you're going to realize as you read this book is that nothing you're going to learn how to do is really that much different from what you do already – it's just going to be a lot easier.

I figured this out when I discovered online marketing around 2008. I had started in commercial real estate finance and development in 1982 and had raised over half a billion dollars in equity strictly through in-person meetings.

SYNDICATE

The process used to look much like this and it's probably something you are very familiar with:

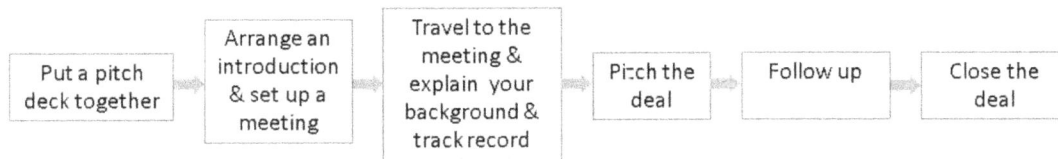

Put a pitch deck together → Arrange an introduction & set up a meeting → Travel to the meeting & explain your background & track record → Pitch the deal → Follow up → Close the deal

First you put a pitch deck together, print it out and make a bunch of copies. Then you'll go to some networking events or arrange an introduction and set up a meeting with a prospect – having little or no idea if they would really pan out or not.

Next you travel to the meeting and go through the whole dog and pony show of explaining your background and track record. Eventually you get around to pitching your deal.

Once that's done, there is an interminable series of follow-ups before actually getting contracts signed and money wired from the investor.

All very laborious and time consuming as you know.

PLUS, you never know if the person you're spending time courting is ever going to actually invest so you have no clue if the time you are spending is worth the effort.

If you could automate this process and meet and greet thousands of prospects in the same way and wait until *they ask you* if they could invest, you'd do that in a heartbeat.

Well you can, and this is how you do it…

Don't print your backgrounder and pitch deck out:
Digitize it

Moving online means you do the exact same thing as in the offline world, only instead of printing on paper your background info and pitch deck, and meeting people in person, you digitize everything so you can automate the whole process:

Here's what that looks like this:

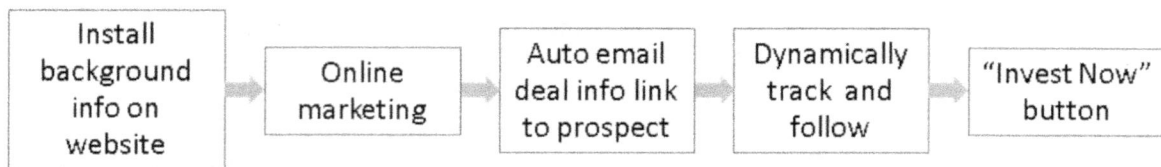

Install background info on website → Online marketing → Auto email deal info link to prospect → Dynamically track and follow → "Invest Now" button

Instead of delivering your background information in paper format, you install it for easy access on your website. Get your message out by posting online instead of physically going to networking opportunities and automate the responses when someone asks for more information.

Using data analytics, you can accurately track and follow prospects' interactions with your content allowing you to respond with such precision you will be able to dynamically adjust your communication with them according to their level of engagement with you.

In the same way as you read a prospect's non-verbal cues – their facial expressions and body language – during an in-person meeting, so you can read their reaction to your online content *allowing you to tailor you communication with uncanny refinement.*

It will seem like you are reading their minds, allowing you the same finesse you are used to when you meet a prospect in person.

And instead of closing the deal with them in-person at a closing ceremony, you'll offer an INVEST NOW button that makes the entire process as easy for your investors as buying a book on Amazon.

Part II: A Blueprint For Success

Here's what we're going to be covering in this book.

1. **A Framework for Building Your Investor List** *where they come to you* so you don't have to go out and find them.

2. **Investor Relations Automation** so you can develop a relationship with prospects without actually having to meet or talk to them.

3. **The Perfect Positioning Process** which is a formula for honing your messaging to make it so compelling to investors that they become predisposed to investing with you before you even pitch a deal.

Now, look, I know that the idea of raising money from investors online without actually having to meet or talk to them sounds implausible.

In fact, I had a comment in one of my Facebook ads recently where somebody posted 'LOL,' basically ridiculing the idea.

And I totally get it because…

This is brand new to commercial real estate.

Indeed, I was also skeptical when I first heard about raising money online to finance deals – but not a little intrigued having always believed there must be a better way to pitch investors.

> You are ahead of the game – raising money ONLINE for real estate has only been allowed since around 2014

To find out more, I contacted all of the early adopters around 2014 which was at the time online marketing for commercial real estate was first permitted, and, on my podcast, I interviewed all the early leaders in the industry who were actually raising money online.

I started to track what they were doing, watching what they were doing, learning how they did it, and *building the same systems for my own website.*

As you know, developers have for generations only ever raised money from people they knew personally, and it was most always done in in-person meetings.

That was exactly how I had always raised money for real estate and how sponsors have all raised money.

UNTIL NOW…

Fast forward to today and the *growth of the industry looks like a hockey stick on a chart.*

You have companies like CrowdStreet who have raised over $1 billion dollars in equity alone from investors, RealtyMogul who have raised over $500 million, Origin Investments who famously raised $105 million in 17 hours for one of their funds, Fundrise, who are said to raise between $1 million and $2 million a day.

Imagine that.

And some of our clients who **raise tens of millions of dollars** without ever meeting an investor.

Just think about the very process that brought you here.

Maybe you saw an ad, maybe you received an email, you saw a post on social media, whatever it was, *chances are you and I didn't meet and I didn't ask you in person to buy this book.*

By very virtue of the fact that you are reading this book proves that this is how people consume information online and can develop a relationship with someone they've never met.

But This is NOT for Everyone

Now, before we go any further, I want to be clear on a few things.

What I'm going to be showing you is very powerful, very effective, but it's not for everyone.

If what you're looking for is a system to make a quick buck or to raise money from investors without having a good deal flow, not only is this book probably not a good choice for you, but you won't raise any money either – certainly not with any kind of long term potential to change your life by helping you scale and build a real estate portfolio.

It might sound obvious, but you need deals to show prospects when you're raising money, and that means deal flow with good terms that are attractive to investors and an ability to deliver on the business plan that you put in place.

The reason my private clients do so well is because they have good deals to put into the systems that we build for them that **make money consistently for their investors time and again.**

Otherwise, if you don't have deals to invest in, you could build the best equity raising mousetrap in the world, *just like you're going to be learning how to do in this book,* and you won't raise a single dollar because you won't have anything of substance to put into it.

Now, that said, you don't want to wait until you do have a good deal before implementing what you're going to be learning because **then it's going to be too late.**

You need to get ahead of the curve and start finding investors before you need them.

AND please keep in mind that any numbers that I share with you from other sponsors or platforms are just by way of example, are largely driven by the caliber of the deals and the sponsor and is not a suggestion that everyone or anyone else can replicate these numbers.

> Don't wait until you have a good deal before implementing what you're learning in this book – because then it will be too late.

Now, the second thing is that what we are going to go through might look easy, but *to build a system that works efficiently so you can raise money on autopilot does take work and patience.*

It is for you if you're committed, motivated, ambitious and confident that real estate syndication is the right business for you, then you're going to love the lessons coming up especially if you're willing to put in the effort and are passionate about being successful.

Works for ALL Kinds of Real Estate

Plus, it doesn't really matter what kind of real estate you're into.

The systems in this book work for just about every single real estate asset class that there is.

In fact, what you are learning has already been applied to just about every (non-real estate) industry out there and is **only just now coming to real estate syndication.**

> It doesn't matter what kind of real estate you invest in, the systems in this book work for EVERY type of real estate.

Here are some of the real estate asset classes this will work great for:

- Fix and flip single family houses, Multi-family apartments
- Industrial buildings, Office buildings
- Self-storage
- Senior housing, Student housing
- Medical office buildings
- Retail
- Hospitality
- Mobile home parks
- Even cannabis or other agricultural real estate

In fact, I cannot think of a single real estate asset class or type that this won't work for if you need to raise equity.

That said, there are a couple of *structures*
that make it harder and require some finesse.
*These include raising money for a **fund or ground-up.***

Funds are harder because the entire process of online capital formation is about education. You have to educate prospects on who you are, your background, and what you do, so by **adding the complexities of fund investing you add another educational hurdle to clear.**

Ground-up projects are also more challenging than others because *most real estate investors want to see passive income checks coming in as soon as they invest.* Unless you have alternate income streams that you can use to finance ongoing passive income for investors, you must clear that educational hurdle also.

Neither are impossible, they just require a little extra effort.

How I Learned to Love Raising Money Online

Fact is, I actually stumbled into the online world by accident.

My real estate career started when I was pulling wires for an electrician 100 years ago and I spent over 30 years raising capital in in-person meetings.

In 2007 I was fortunate enough to have been utterly paranoid about the market and I sold out my entire portfolio right before the *Global Financial Crisis* kicked in and wiped so many developers out of business.

I was hired into a bank through
the Board of Directors where
I built automation systems to handle
the volume of emails that I had to deal with
to sell their distressed portfolio
of real estate.

At the time I didn't know I was building automation systems. They'd not been invented then but I knew that I needed to have systems in place to add more hours to my day.

I sent over at 60,000 emails in the first year at the bank, which might not seem like that many, but I was using a steam powered system that still required a lot of manual inputs.

Out of the bank, I was hired by Gaw Capital to run a $200 million fund to acquire distressed real estate, and from there moved on to Colony Capital, where I did another $100+ million of transactions, primarily structuring real estate collateralized loan portfolios and selling them to investors and banks.

Once the market improved after that downturn, I moved my offices into a startup incubator surrounded by young kids (late teens early twenties) who are all pitching me on their **startup deals for seed and angel capital.**

And they were speaking a foreign language; a language I didn't understand.

It was the language of digital marketing, of content marketing.

And when I saw the laws change in 2012 with the JOBS Act that allowed developers to raise money online for the first time in history, **I realized that this was an incredible opportunity** – an opportunity to blend digital marketing with commercial real estate, to automate capital formation, to automate the process of raising money.

> They were speaking a foreign language; it was the language of digital marketing.

Now, when I started, I had absolutely zero clue how to do it!

I mean, really zero!

I knew nothing about tech.

The closest I got was a reasonably decent knowledge of how to use the Microsoft suite – PowerPoint, Excel and Word, and on rare occasions Access, and that was about it.

So, in addition to learning from the brainiac students who were pitching me on their deals and learning their language, I also started tracking all the companies run by the people I spoke to for my podcast.

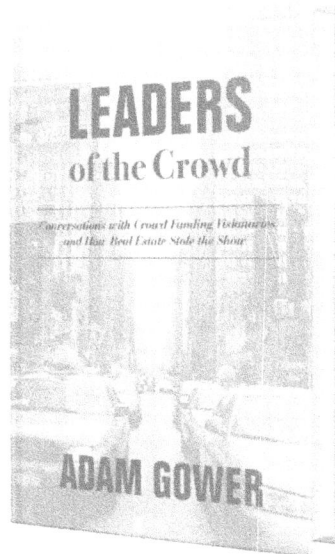

I asked them what they found worked best so I could accelerate my own learning curve. I wrote a book on the subject, *Leaders of the Crowd* (Palgrave Macmillan: New York, 2018) and I started tracking all of the best practices in the industry, building the same systems as they were building and **learning more about digital marketing systems at the same time.**

And, candidly, it was incredibly difficult; I'm not going to downplay that.

But I started to test the systems

on my own website

and through a lot of trial and error

began to crack the code.

And what I realized was that raising money online actually is no different from anything I'd done before.

I was just using technology

to scale it to thousands of times bigger.

All I was doing was taking everything that I had done before, everything that I had in my brain, digitizing it (meaning recording it, creating videos and writing articles) putting it up on my website, and distributing it on social media.

And then I realized that…

You Only Need Three Things to Succeed

When you break the whole 'going online' thing down, there are really only three things you need to be successful:

---

1. **A Post** – on social media to attract prospects by sharing something of value that you have learned.

2. **A Page** – on your website so you can expound further on the topic in your post.

3. **A Form** – so that when a prospect lands on your page they have a place where they can proactively ask you for more information.

Now of course it is more complicated than and we're going to get into the details later in this book, but *the realization that it boiled down to just these three things was totally liberating to me.*

So I decided to share what I had learned with other developers, blending what I knew about raising money for just about every asset class with what I'd learned about content marketing simply because I could tell how powerful and exciting it was and wanted to spread the word.

And by condensing these complicated systems into formulaic blueprints and easy to follow processes so that it would be easy for somebody else to be able to pick up and develop their own capital raising systems, I could actually share what I had discovered, and **save them the entire learning process that had taken me so long.**

Now, fast forward to today, and our clients raise tens of millions of dollars without meeting investors, and their sales process is dramatically reduced because it is all done online using automated systems.

Plus, I see the systems we build working day in, day out on my own stuff.

Seriously, it works like magic.

People call me and say they feel like they know me. *Total strangers.*

And it's exactly what you can do with investors.

It's really incredible how well it works.

Here's The Good News

Now, before I show you exactly *how* it all works and start getting into the weeds, let's kick off with some good news.

One, high net worth individuals inherently want to make more money, no matter how much they have.

They always want more.

They want ongoing income without having to earn it, they want to preserve their capital and they also want to build their wealth without having to lift a finger.

Heck! Everyone wants more money!

And guess what – *that's exactly what you offer in your deals,* so every prospective investor is already subconsciously predisposed to accepting your pitch because they all want more money and that works in your favor.

> Everyone prospect is already PREDISPOSED to accepting your pitch.

Put another way, **you've already got what they want** – you just have to get them to ask you nicely to give it to you ☺

The second piece of good news is that as fabulous and as charming as you are, no matter how great a lunchtime conversationalist you are, and no matter how much you think they do, *your investors prefer not to have to sit with you for a two hour lunch while you pitch them,* just as much as you would prefer not to spend time in person pitching to them.

And that's also good news because if you make it easier for them to learn who you are and about what you do, you'll make it easier for them to accept your pitch…

…without either of you having to go through that traditional mating ritual of an in-person meeting that no one really wants to attend anyway.

You will make your prospects happier about the process and you will **convert that subconscious desire to invest with you into an actual investment** decision where they sign docs and write a check.

And then the third piece of good news, of course, is the silver lining to the whole Covid situation and to *the move to working from home.*

Everyone now working remotely means that there is a huge migration to active investing online, moving it away from the in-person world to the online space.

It is a massive macro-economic, seismic shift to the way everyone conducts business now and **it totally works in your favor.**

But there is some bad news

Before a prospect gets to know you, *they are going to be skeptical and suspicious of who you are and* what you are trying to sell them.

Don't worry too much about that because that's true of anyone (even you) when they're being pitched for anything – but it is something you must address.

You just need to grab their attention with something that stands out and triggers their natural desire for passive income and greater wealth, and then…

…put their minds at rest that you are the right person to deliver those goals.

80% of Success is Showing Up

Your prospects are going to start pay attention to you once they have started to see you around the place more often – which just means you have to elevate your visibility online.

> Just showing up online regularly
> is a huge step in the right direction.

After a prospect sees you a few times online, **you will become familiar to them** and that opens the door just a crack for your prospect to satisfy their curiosity about what you're offering.

It's like the door-to-door salesman of old – except on social media and not at your front door, ringing the bell.

Online, typically someone will need to <u>see your name and brand six to ten times</u> before they'll take a closer look and actually introduce themselves to you.

But when they do…

INVESTORS WILL COME TO YOU

They will introduce themselves to you by giving you their name and email address (the old school business card) as they ask for more information.

Let's look at how you set about creating the ecosystem that enables that to happen.

It's broken down into three core components.

1. **Investor acquisition** where you become magnetically attractive to investors who are drawn to you online and who proactively come to you to ask for more information.

2. **Pitch automation** which is the process by which you capture vital information from your prospects so you can respond with automated emails that they can consume in their own time and that keeps your time free to find deals (or take the day off ☺).

3. **Content multiplier** is how you create a *bait-plume* across the Internet, attracting your most valuable prospects whenever they are out and about online, wherever they are, and in a way that is most convenient for them.

Part III: Investor Acquisition

To get started raising money, you need to be dressed for the part, ready with your calling card and elevator pitch, and this applies as much to the online world as it does as it does to the in-person world.

Online that calls for <u>three types of raw material</u> that you are going to need so you can start building your investor list.

These three things are:

1. **A brand guide (your suit and tie)**

2. **A tagline (your calling card)**

3. **And some e-mails (your elevator pitch)**

Let's go through those individually, starting with the brand guide.

Your Brand Guide

Your brand guide is important because the key to having a successful online presence is going to be consistency. Wherever you show up online, investors need to recognize that it's you, even if subconsciously.

The way you construct that is through your brand guide which itself has three components.

1. **LOGO:**
    o   One, it needs to have a logo that you use on your website and on social media

2. **COLOR SCHEME:**
    o   Two, it needs to have a color scheme is used for all your content, and,

3. **FONT:**
    o   Three, you need fonts that you always use in any written materials.

In the appendices of this book, I have included my own brand guide so you can see how they are structured.

> The key to having a successful online presence is consistency in showing up, and how you look when you do.

Don't copy the colors or logo or anything (duh) but use the format of my guide to create your own. Then go to GowerCrowd.com and to my profiles on LinkedIn and Twitter and FaceBook and YouTube and have a look around to see how, no matter where you are, the GowerCrowd brand is everywhere.

You can create your own brand guide or you can probably find someone at Fiverr.com to create one for you under your guidance.

You Only Have to Do This ONCE

If you spend any time with me, you are going to realize that there are some things I keep repeating because they inspire me so much and I hope they do you too.

Here's one of them.

In the world of raising money for real estate that I have inhabited for almost my entire career and during which I've raised so much equity during in-person meetings, the **one thing that I tired of very early in my career was having to say and do the same thing again and again and again.**

One of the most beautiful things about transitioning to the online world that I love so much, is that *you only ever have to do those repetitive tasks once more and then never again.*

As soon as you record it and put it up online, it does all the repeating for you.

And that's the nice thing about getting a brand guide taken care of.

Once you have it done, you never have to think about what colors to use, what font to use, or how to use your logo.

Now let's move on to the next of your three core raw materials…

Your Tagline

This is a biggy.

This is where you answer the single most important question, in fact the only question that anyone landing on your website is asking, and that is:

WHAT'S IN IT FOR ME – WIIFM?!

Answer that question first and you've got 'em.

Fail to answer that question in the first few seconds that they are on your website, and you may lose them forever.

Your tagline should speak to your core value proposition.

Spend some time researching other sponsor taglines and *make sure yours is unique to you*. Make it aspirational and paint a big picture vision of how a prospect will benefit from spending more time with you.

> Your tagline should paint a big picture VISION of how a prospect will benefit from spending more time with you.

Your tagline is going to appear front and center on your homepage; it is your headline that is **designed to stop a prospect in their tracks and inspire them to read more.**

Here is a great trick for narrowing down what your tagline, your headline, is going to be.

Don't imagine for a moment that you're going to attract everyone.

You are not.

You are however, going to attract people who will love everything you say, who will crave more, who will be ready and waiting to invest as soon as you pitch them, and who will introduce you to their friends and family.

This fan club of yours, are the only people that you need to worry about communicating with.

They are your ideal investors.
Think about your current investors and
put in your mind's eye right now your biggest fan.

This person should be the easiest to raise money from and the most responsive to your pitch AND CRAFT YOUR TAGLINE TO SOMETHING THAT WOULD DELIGHT THAT PERSON – YOUR PERFECT INVESTOR.

Once you have that ideal investor in your sights, everything that you write and produce should be created specifically with them in mind.

Don't worry about anybody else or want anybody else thinks.

Just create your tagline, your brand guide, and all your content to delight that perfect investor and you will be on to a winning ticket.

> *[And if you've ever taught a class of students at university or sat in one of those classes as a student, you know that there are three types of student. There are the deadbeat losers who sits on the back row pretending to be studying but in fact who are watching YouTube videos, there are those who sit in the middle rows who are indifferent to the lesson being taught, and then that all those who sit on the front row, eyes glued to the professor, hanging on every word and who are that group that will work their asses off to get an 'A' grade. THAT is the group that you want to be talking to.]*

Now you have your tagline, next you're going to need a subheading that adds another layer to your WIIFM statement, ideally a benefit of some sort, and a call to action ('CTA' – which, on your home page, leads to a form for them to fill out) where you actively *invite a prospect to join you by asking for their name and email address.*

With these three things, Tagline, Sub-heading, and CTA, you are informing prospects what your website is about, what the benefit to the prospect is of learning more, and are offering an **opportunity for them to actively ask for more information.**

Here are some examples:

RealtyMogul:

Tagline: Invest in Real Estate

Sub-heading 1: Build the future you want

Sub-heading 2: Access institutional quality investments

CTA: JOIN NOW

CrowdStreet:

Tagline: Diversify your portfolio by investing online in commercial real estate.

Sub-heading: None

CTAs: DIVERSIFY EASILY
REVIEW DEALS
TAILORED PORTFOLIO

Fundrise:

Tagline: Welcome to the future of real estate investing.

Sub-heading: Simple, low-cost, and more powerful than ever.

CTA: GET STARTED

Origin Investments:

Tagline: You deserve a better way to invest in real estate

Sub-heading: None

CTA: Explore Our Investments

You'll notice that while everyone has a tagline, not everyone has a sub-heading, and some have more than one sub-heading.

What you will also see is that everyone has a CTA that gives prospects the opportunity to proactively reach out and ask for more information.

There are two basic rules for the CTA.

One is it should stand out from the page
so it should be a separate bright color
to contrast with other colors on the page.

And two, it should include some inviting language, such as

Sign Up

LEARN MORE

GET STARTED >

GET INSTANT ACCESS

INVEST NOW

or any of those given as examples for the various sites in the page above and should be tailored, again, to your unique value proposition and positioning.

In a nutshell, the premise for how to grab someone when they land on your site is to using your tagline, sub-heading, and CTA to do these three things:

- Tell them what you've got,
  - explain the benefits,
  - tell them how to get it.

Explain what's in it for your prospect as succinctly as possible as all they are doing is glancing at your website for a moment and all they're thinking about subconsciously is 'What's In It For Me?'

The Indoctrination Email Sequence

Now, once you've got your brand guide and tagline, subheading, and CTA done, **the third building block you need is an opening email sequence.**

This is going to be a *minimum set of three emails* that will be *set to go off as soon as somebody completes the lead generation form* from the CTA, in sequential order, the first immediately and then the remainder over the next few days.

These emails might, for example, talk about your background, track record and experience. They might cover your investment philosophy or a unique angle that you have on real estate investing.

These emails must be written with your prospect in mind.

Always provide value.

This might include white paper, an investing guide, a case study, or an eBook, for example – and you can use these to entice someone to complete the lead generation form behind your CTA.

> 'Sign up and get our
> free guide to
> multi-family investing.'

The single most important thing to keep in mind is that whatever you send them should continue to be **educational material that delivers value to your prospects** to build trust and inspire them to want to reciprocate your selfless kindness.

Start Building Your Investor List

Once you have your building blocks in place, it's time to build the infrastructure of your lead generation machine, and the way you do that is to **build what is called in the content marketing world as 'a funnel.'**

There are two foundational parts of a funnel:

1. Your Website

The first thing you need is a website, obviously, and your website is going to include your tagline, sub-head, and CTA.

It will be fully branded throughout, and your first set of auto-emails are plugged in, ready to go as soon as someone completes the lead-generation form behind your CTA with their name and email address.

2. Your Social Media Profiles

The next thing is to go ahead and build out your social media profiles.

This is your <u>rent free digital real estate;</u> massive billboards on the information super-highway for all to see!

The main social media platforms to concentrate on at first are LinkedIn, Twitter, Facebook and YouTube.

> Social media profiles are your
> RENT FREE DIGITAL REAL ESTATE; massive billboards
> on the information super-highway for all to see!

Importantly, make sure that the banners you have on these platforms all have a similar look and feel to your website.

In fact, they should use the same graphics and certainly they should use the same branding as you have on your website.

This is so that when somebody lands on any of your social profiles or on your website, **they know they are with you** because it is all tied together by your branding to seamlessly connect all your messaging.

Your tagline and sub-heading also want to be visible on your social channels so you are continuing to speak to your value proposition there also.

Using these on social will speak to why somebody should want to…

migrate from your social profiles

to your website

where you can capture their name and email

address.

Build a FUNNEL to Channel Prospects

The way a marketing funnel works is that the largest number of people enter at the widest part of the funnel, at the top.

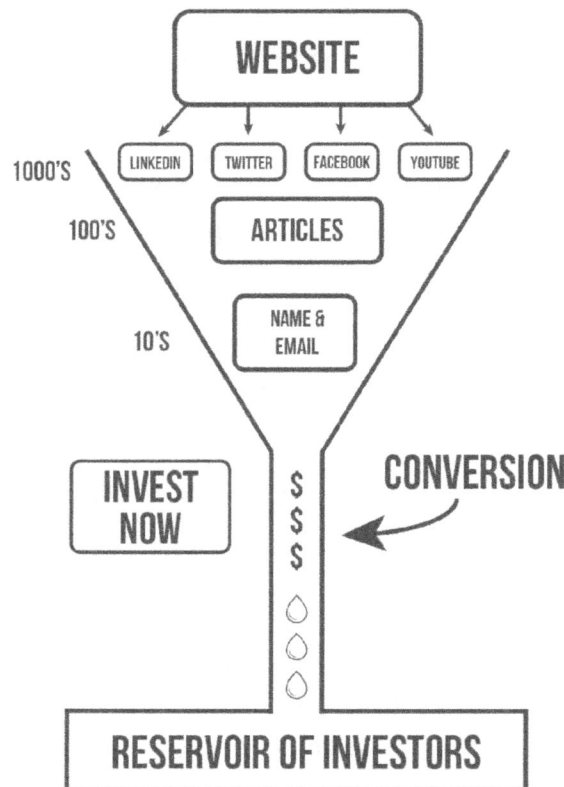

Diagram: A Marketing Funnel

This is where you cast your widest net and where prospects begin to enter your network as they start their journey through your funnel. This is the first part of how you start building your prospect list.

At this uppermost part of your funnel, this is where you are start by creating a 'bait-plume' of content across social media to attract prospects.

The way to do this is **to post links to articles on your website onto your social media channels using short summary posts** that ALWAYS include CTAs saying 'to learn more, click here' or 'watch the video here' if you are posting a link to a video page on your website. (We'll get into how to do that later in this book).

Now, the reason that this is shaped like a funnel is that there are (tens or hundreds of) thousands of people who see your social media platforms and who see your posts in your feeds and this is where the largest audience of prospects are going to start seeing you.

Then a certain number of those will click through to your website from your post and the number of those folk is going to be a factor less than those who simply see the content.

Then there are even fewer who self-select as being interested in you and what you are saying and who tell you that they are interested in knowing more by completing the lead generation form on your website, i.e…

**…by giving you their name and email address
and authorizing you to start sending them emails.**

These are your proverbial students, seated on the front row, eating up everything you are saying and putting their hand up because they have a question and are wanting an 'A' grade.

They are your opt-in leads – your 'hotlist' of prospects – and each time someone does that, *your prospect list gets bigger.*

To give you an idea of how this works, within the first year or so of launch, the GowerCrowd website was getting approximately 200 visitors per day (that's 6,000 per month) and **on a good day we were converting up to 15 prospects** – meaning they completed a form with their email and name and asked for more information.

That's a 7.5% conversion rate, which is pretty good.

We also find that, although it does vary somewhat, *LinkedIn tends to beat out Facebook in terms of how much traffic it sends to our site.*

At time of writing this book,

1. LinkedIn is sending 43.06% of social media traffic to the site,
2. Facebook 41.40%,
3. Twitter 11.88% and
4. YouTube heads up the remainder of assorted social channels with 2.11%.

Keep in mind that we are **posting the exact same content on each of LinkedIn, Facebook, and Twitter** at the same times of day, so these numbers are good comparative indicators of what is possible for traffic for syndication.

When They Sign Up, Immediately Send Prospects An Email Sequence

As soon as a prospect gives you their name and email address using one of your CTAs, you can (and must) start communicating and the first thing you're going to send them is the initial indoctrination email sequence that you pre-wrote and set in place to go out automatically.

This is where the rubber meets the road because once you have someone on your email list, you can start to track their every move. You can see:

- What emails they opened.
- What links they clicked in the emails.
- Which of your social media channels they visited.
- What articles they read.

- How long they spent on your website.
- What pages they visited and in what order.
- What they had for breakfast.*

* I'm just kidding about being able to see what they had for breakfast (though when you start running paid ads you can get pretty damn close to that too).

> Convert an 'invisible' prospect into a 'visible' one with a name and email address you can communicate with

Now that you have converted an invisible prospect i.e. someone who's just circling your website and running searches on you before introducing themselves via one of your CTAs, into being a visible prospect, i.e. someone who's name and email address you have, you can now start to *tailor your communication with them to accelerate their journey to getting to know, like and trust you enough to invest with you.*

Then Ask Them to INVEST NOW

Then there comes the all-important moment which is when you **move from educating your prospects to actively inviting them to send you investment capital.**

And when someone invests, they move to the neck of your funnel, which, at the end of the day, is the only part of it that really matters – when they sign contracts and wire money.

Here's something really important to keep in mind.

This may seem like a long process just to get to the point where you actually ask somebody to invest.

However, pause for a moment and reflect upon what it is that you are actually doing and put it in the context of the in-person process you are used to.

When you are raising money in person, the first thing that you will likely do is to ask somebody for an introduction.

That person might be an attorney, an accountant, wealth manager or an existing investor. They make an introduction for you and you schedule an appointment to meet that prospect.

Well, when you meet a new prospect, what is the first thing that you do?

Whatever that is, the first thing you do at a first meeting
is not handing over set of investment contracts
and wiring instructions
and asking a prospect to 'Invest Now.'

Of course not. The first thing you do is you talk about your background, your track record, and your unique approach to real estate investing.

That's exactly what you do online also – only, as I've shown you, you automate the process, saving both you and your prospects a lot of time (especially you ☺).

So now what happens at this particularly exciting key moment in your investor acquisition funnel when someone signs and wires, is that **your reservoir of investors just grew by one more person.**

This is your active investor base.

And over time, this just continues to get bigger and bigger and bigger.

But That's Just The Beginning

The whole investor acquisition process starts with **your mothership which is your website and from there your prospects' investor journey begins:**

➢ Powering prospect traffic to your website are your brand and messaging consistent social media profiles where the majority of people gain first (and then continuous) exposure to you and your company.

➢ These folk then start to get to know you better because they're seeing you more regularly, recognizing it's you from your branding even if they fly past your post as they scroll down their feeds.

> ➤ They start to consume more information, first clicking on a social media post, and then opening and reading articles on your website, watching videos, and getting emails and newsletters and the like from you.

> ➤ Until eventually you invite them to Invest Now.

Now once you've built this investor funnel – **BUT NOT UNTIL IT'S UP AND RUNNING** with lots of great, high value, educational content on your website – once you've done that, then next, *it's time to start turning up the volume on lead generation*

Your website and social media profiles are just the beginning, the foundation upon which your investor acquisition system is based.

Once you have those in place and content whirring through your machine, then we get to…

…the part where I get all tingly with excitement

because this is where you can really juice your system, drive traffic and find amazing, highly qualified prospects.

This is how you leverage your time and why moving to the online world is so powerful.

Because most of the heavy lifting getting to know prospects in the early phase of relationship development is automated with your marketing funnel:

- ➢ the more attention you can get,
- ➢ the more prospects you will attract,
- ➢ and the more conversions you will make

because it doesn't take any more of your time to scale up.

Remember, you are not going to have to meet everyone (or anyone) so let the system do the work for you and don't fret about how many leads you're going to be generating.

All you need to do is to feed the system with some hi-octane lead generation fuel and below are a few ways you can do that.

They are the...

5 Ways to SUPERCHARGE Your
Investor Acquisition Process

1. Increase your social media post frequency

This isn't as intimidating as it may sound, and you don't have to spend all your time on social media.

Just post the same content multiple times with minor tweaks using an automation tool.

And we'll get into how to easily create lots of content a little later.

2. Host webinars

Webinars are an amazing way to attract hundreds of highly qualified leads very quickly.

You can either automate your own evergreen webinars where prospects can attend at their convenience, or you can hire third party agencies to run them for you.

3. Paid advertising

Between them, Facebook, LinkedIn, and Google can reach every single prospect you would ever want to meet, provided you pay them a fee to do it for you.

Advertising on social media is a science.

It is not to be undertaken without first having a robust online presence.

Your results will be significantly improved that way because as soon as somebody sees your ad, they will want to navigate to your website to find out more about you – so you want to be ready for them when they arrive and greet them with a warm welcome.

4. Public relations (PR)

PR is the process of getting yourself quoted in the right magazines and news feeds, and, if you can, bylines with your name on them (sorry all PR pros reading this for oversimplifying what is a highly skilled job!).

Sure, it's nice to see your name in print, quoted in an article, or with your name on the byline, but again, the first thing someone seeing your name is going to do is to *run a Google search on you,* and travel to your social media profiles and your website.

So, you want to be sure to have the welcome mat laid out for them so you can greet them properly when they show up.

5. Search Engine Optimization (SEO).

I was highly skeptical of SEO when I first heard of it but have come to realize how truly powerful it can be.

Simply stated SEO works like this:

A prospect enters a search term into Google, for example 'how can I invest in real estate?' and Google provides links to articles on websites that answer that question.

That channeling of traffic occurs at **the moment of maximum intent** because it is the moment at which your prospect is actively seeking answers to questions you can provide.

Now, the important thing to keep in mind with these **hi-octane lead generation tools, is that it can only happen only once you have your infrastructure in place.**

There is little point running webinars or paying for ads or conducting PR until you have your infrastructure in place – which means a robust, educational website.

But there is more to it than just that (of course).

Next, we're going to look at the FUNCTIONALITY that you want to have built into your website...

Part IV: How to Optimize Your Website for Conversions

Now that you have your investor acquisition system built, it is time to get your mousetrap set up and properly baited.

We have been building, testing and driving traffic to I don't know how many websites and we've narrowed it down to three key components that EVERY website should have to consistently and predictably capture leads:

---

1. A BUTTON that leads to

2. A FORM, and

3. AN EDUCATION SECTION on your menu bar.

In fact, don't even take my word for it.

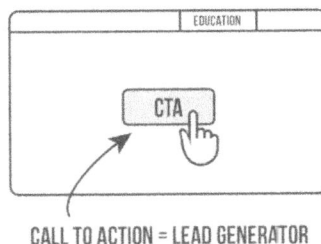

CALL TO ACTION = LEAD GENERATOR

Go take a look at every major real estate crowdfunding website and see if they don't have a button with a form to add your name and email address and an education section on their menu bar of some sort.

Your education menu tab is where you house all the articles and educational articles you produce and is situated on your homepage so prospects can navigate to it quickly and easily.

And there is…

One Big Mistake Almost Every Sponsor Makes

And here is how to avoid that mistake and get ahead of your competition by turning your website into a lead generating MACHINE.

What almost all real estate pros fail to put on their website – and we've already touched on this earlier but I'm going to underscore it here – is a big lead generating button on their home page that says.

LEARN MORE

Or something similar that gives prospects the opportunity to hand over their name and email address.

I mean seriously.

You have gone to all this effort to drive traffic to website – so let's now give it some functionality!

What follows are some **tips and tricks** for some of the finer points of your website's architecture so you can maximize the number of leads you capture, bring them into your network and start nurturing them as soon as they show up to find out more about you.

What to Include On Your Website

1. A CTA Above the Fold.

It is one thing to have a CTA on your home page, and it's another thing to get it in the right place.

We've seen CTAs hidden away on 'contact us' pages, at the bottom of home-pages, or, remarkably, nowhere to be found.

Get a CTA right bang in the middle of your home page where it can be seen instantly by someone lands on your website and before they start scrolling down the page.

This is the most important real estate on your website and is similar to the headlines in newspapers of old that were folded and stacked.

Only the headlines that were above the fold were visible on it and that was what sold the newspaper.

2. Shout out Loud!

Make sure that the color of your CTA contrasts with the background image colors that it is sitting on.

Your call to action needs to stand out because it is important always to *guide prospects through the process by taking them by the hand and showing them exactly what to do next.*

3. Say it Right

There are some classic words or phrases that have been proven to lead to more clicks and conversions than others so don't reinvent the wheel.

Among the best performing CTA language are these:

- Learn More
- Sign Up
- Join Us
- Gain Access
- Join Our Waitlist
- Invest Now

Which of these you use will depend on the stage of raise that you are at but use one of these as you get started – they are among those proven to work best.

Keep in mind that there is little point having an 'Invest Now' button if you don't have something for a prospect to invest in.

You would be better using the 'Join Our Waitlist' option, if, of course, you actually have a wait list.

The other thing that is nice about the online world is that you can test different language to see what works best for you.

So start with something, see how well it converts, and then test something else to see if it converts any better.

4. Offer IMMEDIATE Value

One of the most powerful tools in marketing throughout history has been **the free sample.** *Unfortunately, as a real estate developer, you can hardly go around offering free samples of buildings or even of shares in buildings.*

Therefore, you have to be more creative and the way to do that is to offer free access to valuable information that relates directly to the kinds of deals that you are investing in and raising money for. This might include:

- a white paper.
- a case study,
- an investment guide,
- an eBook
- or other similar high value content.

You can use any of these types of content as click bait in social media posts –

'Click here to get your guide to real estate investing,'

and also as part of the language you can use on your website CTAs, for example,

'Sign up to our educational newsletter and claim your copy of our white paper on investing for success.'

Educate to Motivate

As we discussed, you can't very well be handing out free samples of real estate for prospects to test before investing but you can substitute that for high value content – **which comes with a secondary benefit.**

Like the way free samples of a product work, providing 'free' insights and educational material to prospects creates a *natural human reaction to want to reciprocate.*

The more you give, the more your prospects want to reciprocate because by selflessly giving, you break down the skepticism they feel when they first hear about you.

Put another way, the more they hear from you and about you and your investment philosophy, the more comfortable and settled they become with the idea of taking a risk investing with you **because their perception of risk is reduced the more you communicate.**

Here's an example of how that works.

In the aftermath of World War II, the German army laid minefields as they retreated that needed clearing by the Allied forces.

Prior to clearing these fields, they were sign-posted to keep people out.

The Allied forces discovered that if the fields were marked with the simple legend **'Danger: Keep Out,'** rather than **'Danger <u>Mine Field</u>: Keep Out,'** people were less likely to get blown up attempting to cross them.

> The perception of risk is reduced the more you communicate with prospects and investors. This reduces the barriers to investing and predisposes people to investing with you.

Why?

Because the more people understand about a risk, the higher the likelihood they are going to take that risk because they become familiarized with tactics for mitigating it.

It was the *fear of the unknown* that kept people out of minefields labeled simply 'Danger: Keep Out,' and a belief that they could navigate the field safely that drew people to try to cross them when they were posted, 'Danger Mine Field.'

By sharing information of high value that demonstrates your ability to mitigate risk, you build trust and credibility with a prospect reassuring them that you are not a fly-by-night operator and that you know what you're doing.

Not only that, but you also…

Establish yourself a thought leader

So, *install a link on the menu bar of your website that connects prospects to all your educational content* and that makes it easy for them to access.

Part V: Virtuous Circle of Communication

Now let's connect the dots between everything we've been talking about and start building your email list of prospects.

First thing to do is to...

Grab your prospects' first name and email address

When somebody clicks on your main lead generating CTA on your home page, you are going to want to have your form pop-up and ask for two things.

- First name
- Email address

You want to **keep your form as simple as possible for somebody to complete.**

> Keep your home page lead generation form as SIMPLE AS POSSIBLE for somebody to complete quickly.

You can gather more information about them over time, one step at a time, but to start with all you need is a first name (so you can address them in emails by name) and email address (so you know where to send your emails (duh)).

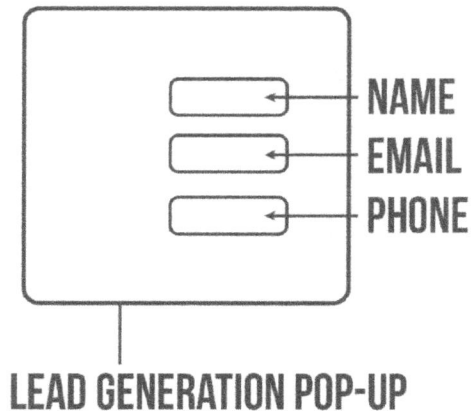

LEAD GENERATION POP-UP

Get their phone number later.

Ask if they are an accredited investor later.

And we like **pop-up forms** because we are getting around 35 percent conversion rates for pop-up lead generation forms on the home page.

Loosely translated, this means is of everyone who clicks on the CTA with the lead generation form, the number of people who complete the form can run as high a 35 percent by giving you their name and email address – which is a very high conversion rate.

And this is where the virtuous circle of communication starts

Now, as soon as a prospect completes the form, it is time to *start communicating regularly and consistently by sending them emails – automatically.*

Each email that you send will have been written in advance and each one needs to contain educational content that benefits the recipient.

Your first sequence of emails, *your indoctrination sequence,* should have at least three emails that you can set to send sequentially over anything from three days to three weeks.

Provide Value

The first thing to talk about is who you are and your background – but not like a resume, or an ego piece about how great you are.

Instead, teach something you have learned that demonstrates how your experience has informed your view of the world *in a way that provides the recipient with a different perspective.*

Create an article or video with this 'lesson' in it. get it up on your website, and in the email sequence you send out, and *write a teaser in the body of your email with a link back to the page with the article on it.*

That way you can track who's opening and reading your emails, whether they click through to the article you're pointing them to, and then track what other pages they go to and how long they spend on your site.

Talk about what you already talk about

Figuring out what this indoctrination sequence of emails should cover is not as difficult as it may seem.

Why not?

Because it's just going to cover same kind of content that you would normally give to somebody in person when you first meet them.

Picture that first meeting in your mind right now and think about what you would most likely talk about and say to put your in-person prospect at ease and wanting to know more – *and talk about that.*

You could talk about your background, how you see the industry, why you like the asset class that you're in, and we'll talk about how to decide what to talk about in a moment, but here's what's important about that.

All this content is going to be situated on your website in your education section in a series of pages so be sure to…

Break Your Story Down Into Bite Sized Pieces

You want to have as many educational pages as possible on your website that speak to your investment thesis and the way you do this is to break down your value proposition into individual small components using *a process called 'content factoring'* (coming up…)

Rather than spending two hours with a prospect over lunch, provide what they want to hear in easy to swallow pieces that they can consume online in their own time.

And share it all on social media

Take the same content, and post it on social media, specifically on LinkedIn, Twitter, Facebook and YouTube.

And, not to worry, you don't have to spend all your life online because you can **fully automate your social posting too (isn't it a wonderful world!).**

Here is a great hack for amplifying your social media reach.

For each article on your website, **you can create potentially dozens of individual pieces of content** to post on social media.

Select single sentences or quotes from the article and create a social media post from just those.

Add an eye-catching image to the quote, brand it properly (colors, logo, font) so even if somebody is flying past your post in their feed, your brand is still registering in front of them and they're still seeing it.

And, of course, include another CTA in the post that does what?

Correct!

Redirects your prospect right back to the article on your website.

That has another CTA, another call to action that asks them to give you their name and email address.

This works fantastically well for gaining visibility online, on social media, for capturing leads, and for staying in front of prospects who have already signed up to your email list.

Part VI: Content Factoring

Now all you need to do is to create high value content laser focused on your unique value proposition so you can...

Fuel your lead generation machine with content

Building the investor acquisition system is like building a car.

The first thing you need to build is the body of the car – that's your website. Looks nice, is attractive, and has doors you can use to get in – the CTAs.

But it is not going to go anywhere without an engine, and the engine is the way you connect social media to articles to CTA's to lead generation forms to automated email sequences.

So now you have a beautiful car, with a powerful engine, but without fuel it is not going to go anywhere – and in the digital world, *content is what fuels everything.*

How to Attract Your Ideal Prospects With Great Content

You'll need content. Lots of it.

Yet, while the idea of producing masses of content may seem intimidating at first, there are only three steps you need to take, and we are going to go through them in this section.

The three things you need to do to create endless streams of content that will create magnetic attraction to you and your deals are:

1. Selecting your topic list.
2. Squeezing a lot of content from a little.
3. Distribution.

Starting at the top:

How to Decide What Topics to Write About

Before your write about anything or product any kind of content, you must pick the topics that are going to be talking about.

This can be challenging when you first think about it and writer's block is very common.

But I want to show you a great way of breaking it down so that you have a seemingly endless series of topics to talk about that are directly relevant to your unique field of expertise.

Here's what you're going to use for that.

First, when you've finished reading this book, go and grab one of your deal memos, pitch decks or, if you want to be particularly ambitious, you can get out a set of your offering docs.

And before getting started on this practical exercise, don't imagine for a moment that anybody you are going to be communicating with knows anything about real estate.

Assume you are talking to someone who knows absolutely nothing.

How to decide what write about

Now you have your deal memo, pitch deck or offering docs in front of you, **take a look at how they are all structured.**

First, every one of those has a series of:

Main Headings

and those headings are separated out according to your own unique story and style of pitching.

Underneath each of those main headings are

Subheadings

and each one of those headings and subheadings can serve as a topic for you to talk about.

That's a good start.

These are topics that you are used to covering time and again every time you meet a new prospect.

Only now, instead of sitting down for two to three hours in a meeting, which is what nobody really wants to do, you can just **create a piece of content using these exact headings and subheadings as content topics.**

For each one of these topics you can produce individual pieces of content to distribute both on your website and also on social media.

Now, one of the biggest challenges that you are going to have is that *you know this topic better than anybody else.*

And when you know a subject extremely well, it can be difficult to explain it to somebody else because you assume that they know as much as you do.

It is very difficult to imagine that they don't but you cannot make that assumption.

So, here's what you do to identify another layer of great content ideas:

Give one of your offering docs or a pitch deck or a deal memo to somebody that doesn't know real estate (like a spouse or a child) and have them go through it and highlight terms and words that they don't understand.

They will create an *amazing* topic list for you.

And the reason this works particularly well is that you're offering docs and your pitch decks and your deal memos **are unique to you.**

So, when you are pulling out terms and words and concepts from those documents, you are really *creating content from topics that are specifically focused on the way you structure your deals.*

And importantly, when you create content this way, you are the concepts **through the lens of your experience that is unique to you.**

That is exactly what your prospects want to hear.

Anybody can go online and research any of the terminology of commercial real estate.

You'll find a thousand definitions of that right across the Internet in articles and videos.

Everybody's an expert.

The only person who counts to your prospects is *you and your perspective.*

And so when you go into your documents and you extract the words that are in there and you **explain in your own language how you understand these concepts**, that is how you are going to present your value proposition to your prospects.

Between your headings and subheadings and the list of words and phrases that your helper has highlighted, you now have a *comprehensive topic list that you can create content about and that is derived from your very own documents.*

This is your content DNA.

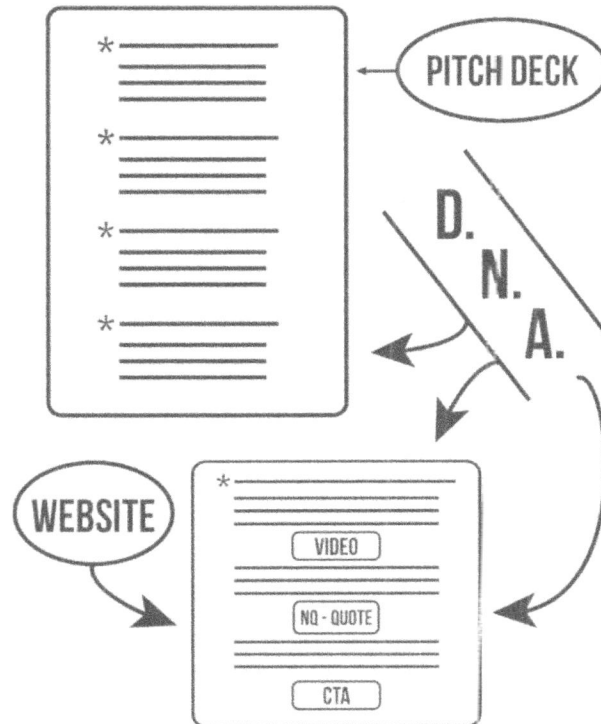

Your pitch deck headings and subheadings become topics for your website content. This is your content 'DNA.'

And this is **incredibly powerful** because by teaching your perspective in this way, you are training your prospects to be particularly receptive to your deals when you finally pitch them, because you will have educated them to see your pitch through your eyes.

> This is one way prospects become PREDISPOSED to investing with you.

It is now time to put some high-octane fuel into your investor acquisition MACHINE and that means that it is time to start creating content.

The more content you have, the more you can push out on social media, the most people see it, and the more leads you get

But how do you create any content, let alone a LOT of content.

That's coming up next...

Be seen everywhere, by everyone, all the time

There are three primary ways to get your content produced:

1. Produce videos,
2. Write articles,
3. Produce 'Notable Quotables'

And all three of these types of content come together in a process called **Content Factoring** where you take one piece of content and create a mass of content from that.

Now, the reason I mentioned video first in the content production chronology above, as counter-intuitive as that might seem, is that your best bet is to start with one of the topics that you've come up with. switch on Zoom and record a video of you teaching that topic.

Or you can use a telephone recording tool, dictate a lesson into your phone, and convert those recordings into video.

Either way, whichever route you choose to go, get the audio transcribed – we use Sonix.ai to do that – and edit the transcript into an article.

From the article, and this is what I love to do, go through that and pick out sentences that are particularly profound ideas that you come up with and those become Notable Quotables.

You see these all the time on LinkedIn or Twitter or Facebook; someone quoting Warren Buffet or Bill Gates or some other famous person.

Well, who is the most important person to your prospects?

You are!

So quote yourself in a post and in the post include a CTA that points to the main article on your website.

Using this technique, from any single article you should be able to get upwards of a dozen Notable Quotables and, whether you've recorded video live on camera or audio to video, you should be able to get around the same number of short video segments as well.

Just take a look at the GowerCrowd podcast series 3 to see how we take one long video and break it down into multiple shorter ones.

It does NOT take much time to create content

Figure it this way.

In normal conversation you are speaking at around 150 words per minute.

If you speak for ten minutes, that's 1,500 words, so a ten-minute video is going to yield an article of around that length, 1,200 words, allowing for editing.

If you speak for half an hour, that's 4,500 words, which would be a long form article (and great for SEO by the way).

Now let's do some basic math.

From a 30-minute recorded teaching session using a telephone recording tool or Zoom for video and creating content in this way by factoring the content that you've got; you could end up with:

- 1 article
- 8 short videos
- 12 Notable Quotables

That's 20+ pieces of content
from just one concept from your topic list.

Isn't that incredible!?

Multiply that by as many topics as you have and very quickly you can be creating a mass of content – certainly enough to reach critical mass very quickly.

Finally, once you have created all this content, what happens next?

Well, of course, you need to start distributing that, so it is time to…

Put your content to work for you

The first place it is going to go is on your website.

Your main articles will each have their own page under the education menu tab.

Include some of your videos in those and some of the Notable Quotables to break the page up from being one huge, long, intimidating block of text.

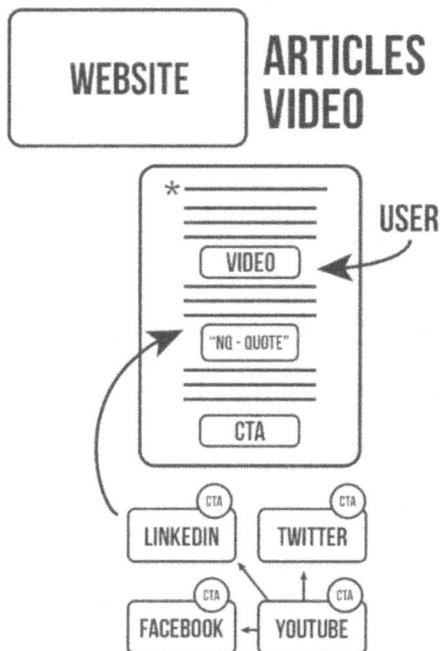

Designing your articles this way is phenomenal for user experience and so, hey, guess what, that means **your prospects are going to spend more time on your website reading more of your content and learning more about you.**

And as a side benefit, *Google also loves that so will reward you by sending high-intent prospect traffic your way (SEO).*

And a really nice thing about having video embedded in your articles is that it allows a prospect to click on a link on social media because they want to learn more, land on the article page on your website **then see you actually talking about that topic**.

Now you have all this amazing content – articles, videos, Notable Quotables – you can get posting it all on your branded profiles on LinkedIn, Twitter, Facebook and YouTube.

Yes!

Get your videos on YouTube, put some post language and CTAs in the comment section for the video and then post links from YouTube directly to social media.

And this whole machine
BECOMES AN ASSET TO YOUR COMPANY

In a nutshell, that's how to produce and distribute really killer content that is directly related to your value proposition to drive the perfect prospects to you who will actively self-select and ask you for more information.

They will see something on social media, and they will say to themselves, that's for me!

And one final thought on this before we move on.

There are two really critical things to keep in mind that I cannot overstate so instead I'm going to repeat it here for emphasis.

Number one, all your content must be informative; it has to add value to your prospects' lives in some way. It must be educational and not just pitch, pitch, pitch.

Number two, the way to create that kind of content is always to keep in mind your prospects' motivations in mind.

Remember, all they care about is 'What's In It For Me' – WIIFM.

Don't just shout about how great you are.

Think about everything that you create from your prospects perspective and provide them with value, with *informative articles that are based on topics that come from your brain and from the way that you conduct real estate, and you will create the best content for them and for you.*

This engine will create a steady flow of well qualified prospects for you for a long, long time.

It has become **an asset for your company** that works day in day out, relentless trawling for prospects, drawing them in, and educating them on how to invest with you.

And once built, this asset will cost you next to nothing to keep in motion and will only stop finding new prospects for you when someone switches the Internet off.

YOUR TAKEAWAYS

Part VII: 7 Action Points to do RIGHT NOW

Congratulations!

You've made it all the way to here and now have everything you need to start building an investor list, raising money, and growing your own personal real estate portfolio so you can build your real estate portfolio and live the life you have always dreamed of!

And what that leaves you with are 7 immediately actionable steps that you can take away and implement right now.

1. **Be sure to install a CTA, a call to action button, right on your website, on your home page.**

2. **Add an education section on your website.**

3. **Create an article and get it up on your website.**

4. **Include a CTA in the article so you can grab name and email address from people that read it.**

5. **Post Notable Quotables from the article on social media**

6. **Be sure to include a call to action (CTA) on the post that points people back to your website or to the article.**

7. **REPEAT ALL THE ABOVE.**

You Only Ever Have to Do It Once

And here's what makes me the happiest about this whole process.

You only have to do it once.

Each time you create a new piece of content that pulls a concept out of your brain and gets it onto your website, it builds on the last one and it continually keeps on getting more and more powerful and effective with each additional piece you add to the machine.

And this is where the magic happens.

As soon as you start factoring your content online, you will start to show up whenever your prospects are online.

You go from being invisible to being visible

And as time goes on and as you post more and more, you go from being just visible **to dominating the dialog.**

And that is exactly where you want to be, because once your prospects see you more frequently, they start to position you as an industry leader and as someone they can trust.

It is really remarkable how this works.

You will also start to gain semi-celebrity status.

I know that sounds ridiculous, but if you implement the lessons in this book properly, people will begin connecting with you and if and when you do actually speak to them, they'll already 'know you' like people know celebrities.

It's the craziest thing.

Total strangers will tell you that they feel like they already know you.

And how does that happen?

Content factoring and online communications.

Now, don't be put off if you have nothing already produced.

The wonderful thing about content factoring is that once you put something up, as I mentioned, it stays there and repeats until you stop it, so when you add something else, your core piece of content just keeps on getting bigger and bigger.

It never gets smaller; it builds on itself.

Don't Wait Another Moment –
Get On It RIGHT NOW!

Build this system out to start drawing prospects into your orbit and here's what's going to happen.

The first people who are going to gravitate towards you are going to be those who have already invested with you or who otherwise are already in your network.

These are your best prospects to start with and your lowest hanging fruit – it is a LOT easier to raise money from people who have already invested with you than from someone for the first time.

By showing up online, *you are reinforcing their trust in you and reminding them in a very gentle way that you are active and leading the field.*

By providing content of high value, you trigger *a subconscious response in prospects that they want to reciprocate in some way teeing them up to being predisposed to investing with you when you ask them.*

This will make it easier for you to raise money, so you don't have to sell as hard when it comes time to actually pitch a deal.

And don't forget, you are pre-qualified to join me in a training recorded live for you where I personally walk you through the entire system so register for that training here or using the link below.

<< REGISTER FOR YOUR FREE TRAINING HERE >>

Now get on out there, build your very own Investor Acquisition System!

HAVE FUN DOING IT AND GOOD LUCK!

Appendix 1

GowerCrowd Brand Guide

gower ➤◄ crowd

Brand Guide

gower crowd

gower crowd

gower
crowd

gower
crowd

Logo Rules

Below are some examples of common misuses of the logo.
Please be sure to use the approved digital artwork and do not
recreate or change it in any way

gower crowd

minimum size for
vertical logo 1.5"

gower crowd

minimum size for
horizontal logo 2"

gower crowd

Do not alter the typeface or
proportions of the name

gower crowd

Do not rearrange the
elements of the logo

gower crowd

Do not tilt or
shift the logo

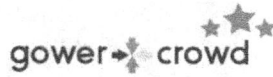

gower crowd

Do not add elements
to the logo

gower crowd

Do not alter the proportions
or change the symbol

gower crowd

Do not change the
color of the logo

Colors & Codes

C 70 M 67 Y 64 K 74
R 35 G 31 B 32
HEX #231F20

C 69 M 48 Y 41 K 21
R 89 G 111 B 123
HEX #596F7B

C 75 M 68 Y 67 K 90
R 0 G 0 B 0
HEX #B9DBD9

C 3 M 2 Y 0 K 0
R 244 G 244 B 249
HEX #F4F4F9

C 88 M 32 Y 81 K 20
R 16 G 113 B 76
HEX #10714E

Typography

TITLES 15pt
COVES BOLD

Sub Titles 11 pt
Merriweather Italic

ABCDEFGHIJKLMNOPQRSTUVWXYZ
abcdefghijklmnopqrstuvwxyz

ABCDEFGHIJKLMNOPQRSTUVWXYZ
abcdefghijklmnopqrstuvwxyz

Body 10pt
Coves Light

ABCDEFGHIJKLMNOPQRSTUVWXYZ
abcdefghijklmnopqrstuvwxyz

Example of Typography:

TITLE
This is a sub-title

This is Body copy. Sed ut perspiciatis unde omnis iste natuserror sit voluptatem accusantium doloremque laudantium, totam rem aperiam, eaque ipsa quae ab illo inventore veritatis et quasi architecto beatae vitae dicta sunt explicabo. Nemo enim ipsam voluptatem quia voluptas sit aspernatur aut odit aut fugit, sed quia consequuntur magni dolores eos qui ratione voluptatem sequi nesciunt. Sed ut perspiciatis unde omnis iste natus error sit voluptatem accusantium doloremque laudantium, totam rem aperiam, eaque ipsa quae ab illo inventore veritatis et quasi architecto beatae vitae dicta sunt explicabo. Nemo enim ipsam voluptatemquia voluptas sit aspernatur aut odit aut fugit, sed quia consequuntur magni dolores eos qui ratione voluptatem sequi nesciunt.

Don't Forget to Claim Your

FREE Training

Taught Personally by Adam Gower Ph.D.

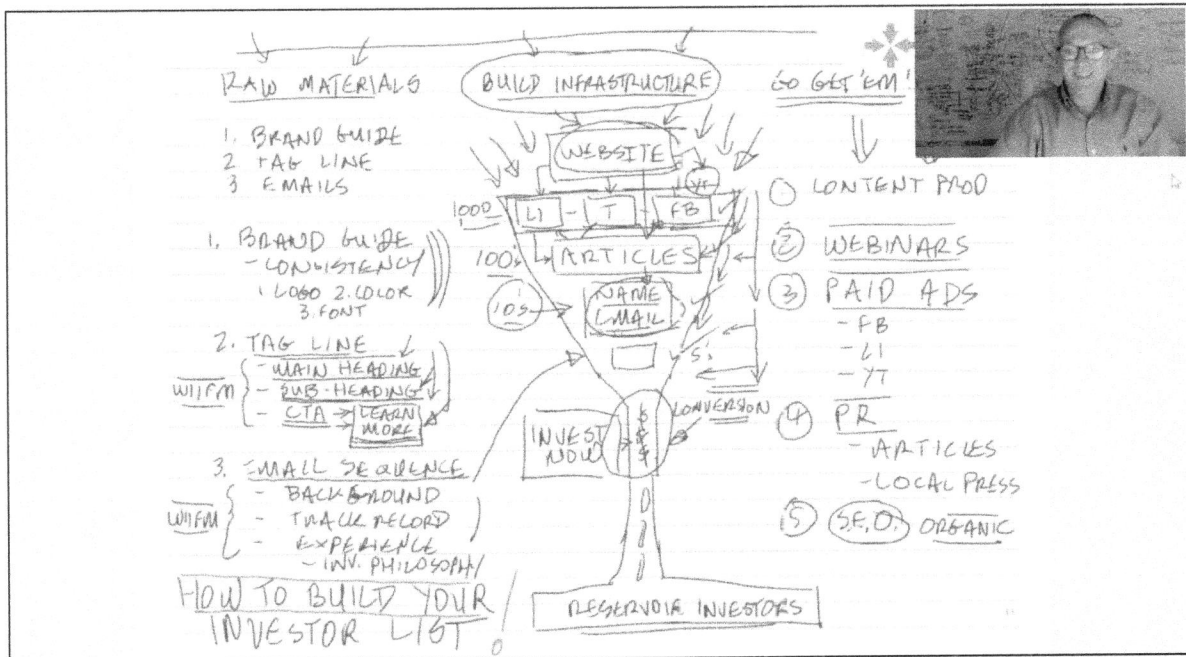

<< Click to Register Here for Immediate Access >>

Or go here:

hub.gowercrowd.com/syndicate-webinar